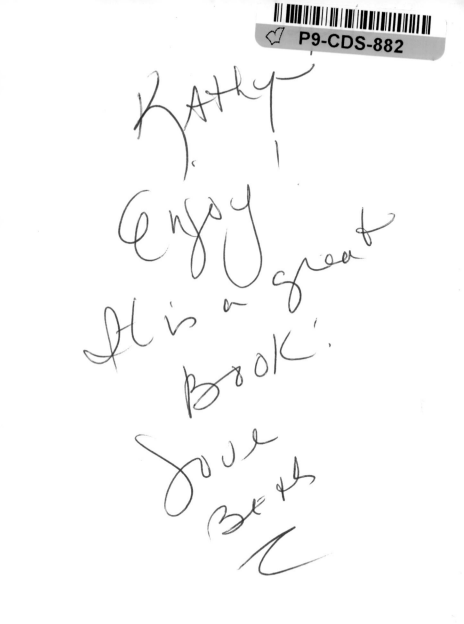

Kathy

Enjoy

It is a great

Book!

Love

Beth

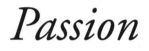

Passion

Passion

Barbara De Angelis, Ph.D.

Delacorte ▤ Press

Published by
Delacorte Press
Bantam Doubleday Dell Publishing Group, Inc.
1540 Broadway
New York, New York 10036

Library of Congress Cataloging in Publication Data

De Angelis, Barbara.
Passion / Barbara De Angelis.
p.   cm.
ISBN 0-385-31435-3
1. Emotions.   I. Title.
BF531.D35   1998
152.4—dc21   97-51854
CIP

Manufactured in the United States of America
Published simultaneously in Canada

July 1998

10   9   8   7   6   5   4   3   2   1

BVG

*This book is offered
with unending love and gratitude
to You who are
the Source
the Path
and the Goal
of my True Passion.*

Acknowledgments

Special thanks to these dear friends
whose unwavering love and steady wisdom
offered me support, clarity, and courage
and made writing this book possible:

Sally Fisher, Pam Kear, Sandy Jolley,
Peter Ishkhans, Wendy Goldstein,
Jackie Eckles, Jennifer Munoz,
and Swami Kripananda.

Contents

PART THREE

Living With Passion

Introduction

I wrote this book as an offering of my own passion for the work I am here to do, and as an invitation to the part of you that knows you are ready to feel more, live more, love more, and enjoy more. So often, people ask me, "Barbara, what is the secret for creating happiness?" or "What is the one quality I need to develop so I can experience true confidence to pursue my dreams?" or "What should I focus on to attract good things into my life?" And my answer to all these questions is always the same: PASSION.

Passion is much more than the intense physical attraction we feel for another person, or a strong belief in a cause, or even an enthusiastic attitude toward our relationships, our work, and our family. It is not just a quality to possess or an emotion to hope for. *Rather, passion is an inner source of energy that is powerful, loving, and benevolent, an energy that, when it is allowed to flow into your life, will infuse each experience, each encounter, with vitality, magic, and meaning.* In this way, to live passionately is a state of *being*, one in which you bring your full heart and soul to every moment of every day.

Passion is what opens us up to life, and opens up the door to life's most precious treasures to us. It takes great courage to live and love with passion, but is there really an alternative for those of us who seek the highest? To experience passion, to express it, to share it, is to give a priceless gift to ourselves, to others, and to the world around us.

These reflections on passion are designed to help you contemplate your own passion in ways that, perhaps, you haven't before, and to offer you new possibilities for becoming the passionate, powerful person you long to be. I hope that as you read, you will be inspired to work with more passion, play with more passion, love with more passion, and grow with more passion. This is the life you deserve to live.

—Barbara De Angelis

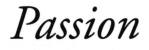

Passion

PART ONE

PASSION:
YOUR ESSENTIAL
SELF

Passion Is the Source of Who You Are

In the beginning, there was passion. Your life, your very existence here on earth, has its source in passion. For at least one moment, passion pulled a man and a woman so powerfully together that they joined their bodies, and from that passionate union, your seed was born. And when that seed grew, and you were ready to enter the world, you did it with all the passion you could muster, your loud cries informing everyone in no uncertain terms that you had arrived!

Your very body is constantly vibrating with passion. How can you call your heart anything but passionate as it beats with unceasing loyalty twenty-four hours a day, every day, every year of your life? How can you think of your lungs as anything but passionate as they faithfully drink in all the air you need, even while you are sleeping? And what could be more passionate than your blood itself, jubilantly racing through thousands of invisible pathways in every part of your body, bringing vitality to every limb and every organ?

It may seem that the passion of your body to keep

itself alive is merely a biological phenomenon. But this same passion that drives you toward a state of well-being is your essential nature, not just physically, but spiritually. It is what allows you to give birth to yourself over and over again. Each new beginning, each inner transformation, each outer change of direction is fueled by your passion for more truth, more happiness, more freedom. Each time you choose to change, to grow, to improve, you are choosing to act from that inner core of passion.

It's your passion that, throughout your life, will be your saving grace, for it will keep you going after your dreams when everyone advises you to give up, keep you searching for the right partner even when you're afraid he or she isn't out there, keep you traveling on the path of self-discovery even when you aren't sure where the road is taking you or even what you are looking for. Ultimately, it will lead you to the destiny that you can already hear calling to you from within your own heart.

*Passion is not a quality that is foreign
to you.
It is not a characteristic
that some people are born with
and some must do without.*

*To be passionate is as natural to you
as breathing,
as natural as being alive.*

It is the source of who you are.

Our Hunger for Passion

The hunger for passion is universal. Something in our human nature longs for that experience of complete emotional absorption, that magical moment when we are swept away, finally free from our everyday rules, restraints, and routines. Each of us, in our own way, seeks to have our passion awakened. Each of us searches for that which will allow us to feel fully vibrant, fully alive.

Have you ever wondered why there are so many sports fanatics who can't seem to get enough of football, basketball, baseball, or hockey, depending upon the season? Perhaps you've observed your own mate shout at the television set and pound the couch, and been amazed at the intensity of his reaction to what, to you, looks like "just a game." What is it that has him so mesmerized that he never goes for more than a few days without watching a game?

Or perhaps you've had a friend obsessed with a daily soap opera, or romance novels. "How can she watch that trash?" you think to yourself. "And those books—don't

7

they all have the same plot and the same predictable sex scenes? Why does she read one after the other?"

This man and this woman might be shocked to discover that, although on the surface they appear to be very different, in fact, they are both craving the same thing: PASSION. When he watches a professional sporting event, what does he see? Usually, a bunch of men running up and down the field, or the court, passionately striving toward a goal with all their energy, all their focus. When she reads her romance novel, what does she come in contact with? Characters leading dramatic lives full of excitement, intensity, and yes, passion.

It is passion that entertains us. When a team plays without passion, the game becomes boring. "These guys are asleep," a fan complains in frustration as he reluctantly switches channels, or leaves the arena early, hoping to go home and catch the end of another, more passionate contest on TV. When a novel is written without passion, you quickly lose interest in reading it. "Nothing's happening," you conclude with disappointment as you put the book aside.

To feed this appetite for passion, we heavily reward those individuals who can stir our emotions to the greatest heights—actors, professional athletes, and rock musicians all make millions of dollars because they know how to turn our passion on. Right or wrong, we place a higher financial value on their ability to stimulate us than we do on the people who teach our children or who grow our food.

There's nothing wrong with admiring individuals or enjoying events that fire up our passion. The problem arises when we don't experience enough passion in our own lives, and try instead to get high off other people's passion. The sports fanatic who gets more excited about watching sweaty strangers bump into each other than he does about spending time with his own wife, the fan of a TV program who feels more emotion for the characters she watches each day or each week than she does for herself, the person who loves reading about other people's dramas and heartbreaks in the tabloid newspapers and avoids facing her own—these are all people cut off from their own passion, their own aliveness, their own life.

If you are in search of your own passion, start by turning away from the quick fixes and contact high you get from people and situations on the outside, and instead, turn your awareness within. Only your own passion will ever truly satisfy you. Only your own passion can never be stolen from you. Only your own passion can make you feel truly alive every moment of every day.

When you rely on other people
to get you excited about life,
you are making them the source
of your passion.

When you depend upon other people
to stimulate you to feel,
you are giving them control
over your aliveness.

Become the source of your own passion.
Become the source of your own aliveness.

Becoming a
Passionate Person

Who are your heroes, your heroines? Whom do you admire? Whom do you wish you could be more like? If you made a list of people you truly respect, people who inspire you, chances are that they would all share one characteristic: PASSION. Some might have tremendous passion for a cause or belief, some might have tremendous passion for their form of artistic expression, others might have tremendous passion for achieving certain goals. But all of them would probably be individuals about whom you'd say, *"He or she is really a passionate person."*

What is so appealing about someone who is passionate? *When we encounter a person who is passionate about the part they play in the world, we are witnessing the life force as it expresses itself fully through this individual.* Whether he's a musician who's passionate about his songs, a spiritual teacher who is passionate about God, or a professor who is passionate about what she is teaching, all of these people are giving themselves fully to life, and life is fully giving itself back to them and through them.

When we call someone "charismatic," what we're really noticing is their passion. Passion is seductive. It is alluring. We are attracted to passionate people. We want to watch them, listen to them, be around them, and secretly or not so secretly become them.

This, then, is the real secret for charming others, for inspiring others, for becoming the kind of person who makes a true impact on the world—discover your passion for life, for love, for what you believe in, and let it shine.

Passion acts like a magnet
that attracts us to its source.

We are drawn to people
who radiate with passion,
who live with passion,
who breathe with passion.

Your passion is your true power.
The more you discover and express
your passion for life,
the more irresistible you will become
to others.

Commitment Creates Passion

Passion is born of commitment. When you are committed to something, whether it's a dream, a cause, or a relationship, you feel passionate about it. And the deeper your commitment, the stronger your passion.

How does commitment create passion? It's the actual inner experience of committing yourself to something you believe in that unleashes your natural passion, your natural enthusiasm, your natural devotion. In that moment when you realize "Yes, I believe in this idea," or "I believe in this person," it's as if your mind finally gives your heart permission to participate fully in whatever or with whomever you've committed to. All of a sudden, you're flooded with more excitement, more energy, more love. The commitment itself acts like a key that unlocks the door to your secret storehouse of passion.

It's very difficult to feel passionate about something when you aren't committed to it. In fact, it's nearly impossible. Think about something you don't particularly feel committed to doing or participating in—a political cause you don't believe in, a project you don't approve of at work, a chore around the house your partner thinks is important that you think isn't necessary. Ask yourself, "Do I feel passionate about these things?" Of course, the answer is a resounding "NO." Your lack of commitment doesn't allow your passion to flow toward these projects. *You simply can't get motivated to care about them and take action on the outside, because you've never committed to them on the inside.*

Try this simple experiment: Choose one area of your life in which you'd like to feel more passion, perhaps your relationship, your job, or your emotional or spiritual growth. Then, for even one day, deepen your commitment to it. If it's your partnership or marriage, express more commitment through your words and your behavior. Focus on the best qualities of your mate, and remind yourself of how much you do love about him or her.

If it's your job, give one hundred percent to each task and each interaction. For instance, if your work involves sales, treat each customer with as much care, respect, and concern as you're capable of. If you're a graphic designer, put your whole being into each sketch, each rendering, as if it will be your greatest masterpiece. If you're a full-time mother, help your child with his homework as if the love you show in that half hour will change the course of his life.

Perhaps you're experimenting with deepening your commitment in an area of personal growth, such as slowing down from your usual hectic pace and appreciating more of life's special moments. Spend a whole day noticing when you're becoming stressed, and remember to take a pause, just for a few seconds. In that time, you can pay attention to what you've been missing—the beautiful trees lining the streets that you usually race by on your way to the office; how cute your dog looks when you pass him in the kitchen as you rush to make dinner; the sound of the night birds and crickets singing outside as you get ready for bed and are already thinking about how much you have to do the next day.

You will be amazed how the act of committing more intently to one thing you care about for just one day can transform your experience of life and of yourself. People who seemed unexciting suddenly become interesting, fun, and attractive. Tasks that seemed mundane and boring become stimulating, and fill you with contentment. Personal challenges that seemed unattainable become opportunities for significant and lasting breakthroughs. Most of all, you will discover that your own passion has been just waiting for a chance to burst forth and express itself.

The more of yourself you offer
to something,
the more passion you will receive back
in return.

Do whatever you do with commitment.
Love whomever you love
with commitment.
Choose whatever you choose
with commitment.

Then, whatever you do will be infused
with passion.
The relationships you have will vibrate
with passion.
The choices you make will resound
with passion.

Passion and Indifference

Indifference is the enemy of passion. It is the enemy of life. When you say to yourself, "I don't care," you not only cut yourself off from someone or something else—you cut yourself off from your own life force, from that source of love and power inside of you.

These days, indifference is almost fashionable. To be indifferent is to be cool, to be unattached to what happens, to be truly independent. Phrases like "whatever . . ." and "I couldn't care less" are heard every day on television, at the office, in schools, and at home. We hear them from our teenagers, from our friends, from our lovers, and most disturbingly, from ourselves.

Indifference is a devious attitude. It can disguise itself as appearing to be other, more desirable, qualities, such as inner strength, introversion, and emotional evenness. "It's not that I don't feel anything," you find yourself insisting to someone who is accusing you of being indifferent. *"I'm just in a very centered place right now, so I'm not reacting much."* When you combine indifference with self-righteousness, it responds even more aggressively by making you right and others wrong: *"Look, just because you are overly emotional and lose control doesn't mean that I have to be that way too. The only reason I look indifferent is because to you, anything less than effusiveness or hysteria is indifference!"*

I know some people who try to excuse their indifference by masquerading it as spirituality. *"I'm not indifferent,"* they proclaim. *"I'm just not attached to anything in the outside world like I used to be."* This is what I call a "kindergarten understanding" of spiritual achievement. History has given us countless examples of saints, teachers, and holy beings who are the embodiment of caring, compassion, and passion, and who could never be described as indifferent. Indeed, the more we contact our divine essence and perceive the truth of life, the more we recognize the inherent oneness of everything in creation, and thus, the more love we feel for everyone.

What, then, is the source of our indifference? *Most of the time, it is fear—fear of pain, fear of loss, fear of feeling too much.* For instance, when we say "I don't care," what we often mean is: *"I don't know how to care without getting hurt,"* or *"I wish I didn't care,"* or *"I'm afraid to care because I know that caring will be more challenging to me than not caring,"* or *"I'm angry that I care so much."* Indifference becomes the armor we choose to wear, hoping to avoid the pain of not being loved in return, or failing at one of our goals, or having to face criticism and disapproval from others.

But don't let your indifference fool you. Never, never does indifference give you strength. Never does indifference protect you. Instead, it creates a wall of numbness and pride between you and that which you long for—intimacy, passion, and the fulfillment of your goals and dreams. *In the end, indifference robs you of your greatest strength, your greatest protection and your greatest blessing— the abundant love and passion that lives in your heart.*

It takes great courage and great humility to face your indifference. Ask yourself:

"Is there any area of my life in which I've been hiding from my fear or pain behind indifference?"

"How have I been numbing myself to people or things I really care about?"

"Where in my life do I need to care more?"

"Whose love, friendship, or kindness have I been taking for granted and responding to with indifference?"

Just this act of challenging your indifference with honesty will instantly wake up your caring and your passion, and begin to break down the walls around the wellspring of love inside your heart.

*Don't allow fear to seduce you
into indifference.*

*Guard your passion
as you would guard
your most precious possession.
Defend it as you would defend
your dearest companion
from harm.*

*You will be rewarded with a life
of grace and exuberance.*

Passion and Control

Are you the kind of person who needs to be in control all the time? Do you get irritated when things are out of place, when the towels aren't hanging straight on the towel bar, when someone parks over the lines, when a glass is left out on the counter, when things don't go exactly the way you planned? If so, you probably aren't experiencing as much passion in your life as you want to, because *passion is what happens when we let go of control.*

Control is really the antithesis of passion. Control approaches situations with rigidity; it likes to confine things to boundaries; it seeks certainty, lack of movement; it resists change.

Passion, on the other hand, overflows the boundaries and seeks no limit, no end. It thrives on the unknown; it feeds off movement and transformation; it adores the uninhibited.

Passion is not necessarily logical, or appropriate—words which are favorites of those who love control. It manifests simply because it wants to. It expresses itself for its own sake. *Its purpose is none other than the celebration of life, of love, of God's creation.*

Imagine that you're hiking in the woods on a cool winter day and you come across an icy, rushing river. Logic calmly tells you that, in spite of how warm you are from the hike, the water is much too cold for a swim, but passion swells up in your heart and shouts: "Throw off your clothes and jump in—now!!" Something within you longs to experience the wonder of life, the gift of nature, the magic of the moment, whether it makes sense to the mind or not. And when you plunge into the water, shrieking with joy as every cell in your body wakes up, you feel completely present, completely alive. *You are out of control, and loving every second of it!*

To enter into the world of passion, we must relinquish our need to predict outcomes and understand exactly what is happening from moment to moment. We must be open to the mysterious, the unexpected, the subtle. We must release our need for our usual expectations to be met, and allow that which is out of the ordinary to reveal itself. We must be willing to let go of control, and adventure into new pathways of feeling, of perception, of experience, pathways that will lead us to more joy and wonder than we could ever imagine existed.

Open yourself to the potential
in this moment.

Let go of how you think
it should look.
Let go of how you think
it should feel.
Let go of trying to control
what is happening.
Just let go . . .

Now, you've created the space
for magic to occur.
Now, you've opened the door
so that the mysterious may rush in.
Now, you've made room in your heart
for passion.

The Secret All Children Know About Passion

All children possess a secret that few adults remember or understand—the secret for living every moment with unedited passion and wonder. Watch a child play and you will see passion in action. Each decision is undertaken with passion; each opportunity is explored with passion; each new adventure is begun with passion; each obstacle is resisted with passion. You can witness this passion shining in the child's eyes, hear it in his jubilant shouts and laughter, feel it in the air around him. He is truly celebrating his existence. He is truly alive.

What is it that allows a child to give so much to everything he does? I believe it is the fact of his innocence. He hasn't yet learned to be self-conscious, so he doesn't worry that the little song he's singing to himself will sound silly to others. He hasn't yet learned to fear failing, so he doesn't care that he has fallen down ten times while trying to learn to roller blade. He hasn't yet learned indifference, so he isn't concerned that he's showing too much excitement about his upcoming trip to the amusement park. Instead of focusing on how he is being perceived, he immerses himself in the sheer joy of being himself.

Children also intuitively know something else about being passionate—it feels good! This is why kids give themselves permission to feel fully. To really laugh, to really cry, to really want something, to really need someone, these are strong expressions of emotion we as adults rarely allow ourselves, particularly when we're around other people. Instead, our natural passion gets pasteurized of its raw essence, and what we experience instead is a kind of guarded participation in our feelings that leaves us lukewarm or even indifferent to much of our world.

If you suspect you've turned into a bored, boring, passionless grown-up just like the ones you swore you'd never become, then perhaps it's time to rescue the child you used to be from the closet of appropriateness you locked him in years ago. Let him or her out once in a while. Allow him to be your teacher. You'll be delighted to find that you will care more, dare more, laugh more, hug more, question more, enjoy more, and of course, feel more passion for every moment of your wonder-filled life!

*When was the last time you let
the passionate part of you
out to play?*

*When was the last time
you had as much fun as your kids?*

*When was the last time
you felt excited just to be alive?*

*Stop worrying about
what other people think,
or if what you feel like doing
is practical, useful, or efficient.*

*Be silly.
Be passionate.
Be yourself.*

Passion and Surrender

Think back to a time when you experienced tremendous passion. The passion could have been physical, emotional, or even spiritual. As you recall that moment of great intensity, you'll notice that while you were experiencing this flood of passion, you also experienced a sense of surrender: you were not in charge of the experience. Something more powerful than you took over, and you surrendered to it. You let go. You allowed yourself to be swept away by what was going on, and from this act of surrender grew passion.

If the experience you remembered was a moment of great physical passion, think about what occurred prior to that moment. You felt waves of pleasure building up in your body until, at some point, the force of those waves became greater than any sense of control you had, and you surrendered totally to the sensation. If you had resisted, if you had been frightened to let go so completely, if you hadn't been willing to surrender, you would have stopped the pleasure from reaching its passionate peak.

Perhaps you recalled an experience of emotional passion, a moment of intense feeling. Maybe it was the birth of your child, or a long-awaited reunion with a family member, or an encounter with someone or something that moved you deeply. Take yourself back and remember how you could sense the emotions building inside of you, becoming stronger and stronger until your heart felt like it was going to burst—and then it did, in waves of joy and ecstasy. It's no accident that this sounds like a description of an emotional orgasm; the process is very similar. You surrendered to the feelings, to how vulnerable they made you feel, and allowed them to grow until they exploded in a profound moment of emotional passion. If you had fought the feelings, you would have successfully shut your heart down, and never experienced such love, such delight.

Many people misunderstand the true meaning of surrender. It is not the same as giving up, relinquishing your power, or losing something valuable, such as surrendering in battle. *To surrender means to get your limited ego out of the way and align yourself with a force more powerful than your will. When you surrender, you let go of whatever is stubbornly holding you in the place you presently are, and flow with the current of the river of life that wants to take you to something greater.*

If the idea of surrender scares you, you probably don't experience as much passion as you could in all areas of your life. Begin to notice when you are resisting surrender, when you are trying to hold your ground, to maintain your boundaries, whether during a conversation, or lovemaking, or a walk in the park, or an encounter with your own emotions. Give yourself permission, a little bit at a time, to take a deep breath and let the force you feel tugging at you from inside take you where it wants to go. In that moment of surrender, you'll suddenly experience a wave of passion wash over you!

Surrendering to your own passion
isn't surrendering to something
or someone
on the outside.

It's surrendering to the power
of your own love,
your own joy.

It's surrendering to your Self.

The Heart Is the Home
of Passion

Passion isn't an idea, it's a feeling. It's not an attitude, it's a way of being. It has nothing to do with intelligence, cleverness, or comprehension. Its home is in the heart.

The true heart I'm talking about here is not a place in your body. It's a state you enter when you are willing to feel, when you are willing to love, when you are willing to be loved. This true heart is the core of who you really are. It is the pulsation of your spirit.

Ironically, most of us don't spend our time striving to cultivate our heart. Society instructs us, instead, to become valuable by getting an impressive job or marrying an impressive person, making money, and accumulating material possessions. Emotional mastery isn't on the list of achievements we're encouraged to accomplish. Our life may be comfortable, and look acceptable to others, but if we're honest with ourselves, we may have to admit that it's devoid of any real, consistent passion. And even though we may want to feel more, we're often not quite sure how to go about it.

If we pride ourselves on being highly intelligent, we may find it even more difficult to experience true passion. People who spend a lot of time in their head aren't usually the most passionate individuals around. If your goal is to be smart or knowledgeable, you will focus your energy on mastering skills, collecting information, and forming conclusions. You figure that the more you know, the happier you'll be. In fact, often the opposite is true—the more you know, the more logical you become, the more likely you'll be to let your mind talk you out of your feelings, out of your passion. The result? You risk ending up dry, hard, and unreachable.

I'm not suggesting that you should become mindless in order to live with more passion. Becoming more passionate *doesn't* mean abandoning the use of your intellect. The mind is a powerful and necessary tool that helps you channel your passion through the vehicles of creativity and communication, and provides balance to your emotions. But too often, we hide behind the shelter of what we know to avoid facing what we feel, and that's when we cut ourselves off from our passion.

If you want to spend more time in your heart, spend more time with people who are in touch with theirs. Haven't you noticed that passion is contagious? When you're with someone whose heart is open, it will be so much easier and so much safer for you to open to your own feelings. Look around—the world is full of people just waiting to dance with you in the magical realm of the heart.

*To find your way back to your passion,
you must first find your way
back to your heart.*

*There, at the center of your being
resides the source of all you are.*

*You are light.
You are joy.
You are love.*

PART TWO

PASSION AND
INTIMATE
RELATIONSHIPS

The Sacred Passion
of the Body

Nothing in the physical realm of relationships is more intimate than sharing the passion in your body with your beloved. This passion is the one part of you that no one else in the world sees, the part that you keep only for him or for her. It is your life force itself, the way your spirit dances in the flesh, and therefore it is sacred. And thus the sharing of your passion in the form of sexual union becomes sacred as well.

Most of us would never place the words "sacred" and "passion" together. We have been taught that passion is a base emotion, synonymous with lust, and that things which are sacred have nothing to do with the body, that they transcend the physical. Yet isn't the physical body simply an expression of spirit? And therefore, isn't sexual intimacy a way the life force plays upon the platform of the body?

If all you are seeking out of your sexual relationship is pleasure, you are shortchanging yourself. I'm certainly not saying that you should bypass the pleasure and the physical passion. Just don't stop there! There is so much

41

more than that available to you. *The natural passion you feel for your partner can be a doorway into a new kind of sexual experience, where you learn to use physical love as an opportunity for sacred communion.*

From this point of view, the sensation of passion is just the starting point in lovemaking. It is the physical expression of a much more timeless, more abstract desire. For hidden in the core of the passion is the longing for union, for total oneness with your beloved. *Your body may be reaching out to touch your lover's body, but in truth, it is your soul that, through the vehicle of your body, is reaching out to touch your lover's soul.*

If you're ready for new and astonishing levels of fulfillment in your relationship, then don't take the passion you feel for your mate at face value. Look deeply into its origins. Talk to it. Ask your passion: "Why do you want to embrace him?" "Why do you want to enter her?" Listen for the answers in your heart. And don't be surprised if you hear the voice of your own spirit whisper: *"To be one . . . to be one . . . to be one. . . ."*

*Passion begins where your bodies unite
and ends where your souls dance.*

*When your spirits can join together
at the same time as your bodies
become one,
then all of you will be making love.
There will be nothing left between you
that is not love.*

*This is sacred communion.
This is ecstasy.*

Emotional Passion

An intimate relationship cannot survive over time on physical passion alone. There must be a strong bond not just between the bodies, but also between the hearts of two lovers. This bond transcends mere sexual attraction. It is a bond of emotional passion between you and your mate.

We all know what it means and what it feels like to be physically passionate about someone. For this reason we usually think of passion as a sensation. So what, then, does it mean to be emotionally passionate about a person? The center of emotional passion is in the heart, not in the sexual organs. It is not based on infatuation, chemistry, or desire. *It is based on a deep recognition of the love in another person, the love in your own self, and the joy these two forces create when they play together.*

You may be able to feel physical passion for someone you don't like very much. After all, lust and love are two different sentiments. *But to feel emotional passion for a person, you have to really like him or her.* You are passionate about your partner's character; you are passionate about his personality; you are passionate about his mind; you are passionate about his spirit. Unlike physical passion, which is born of need, emotional passion springs from an unmistakable resonance you feel with your beloved.

The wonderful thing about emotional passion is that the more moments of love you share with your mate, the stronger the emotional passion becomes. Each day he does something wonderful that allows you to see his greatness. Each day she says something thoughtful that allows you to see her sensitivity. Time becomes the friend of your relationship, as it creates more and more opportunities for your partner to reveal his goodness, his sweetness, his kindness, and thus, more fuel to feed your emotional passion for him.

In the end, it is emotional passion that keeps a marriage together for a lifetime; it is emotional passion that allows a couple to go through great challenges and crises and come out even closer than before; it is emotional passion that makes you feel truly safe and truly loved.

This passion of the heart anchors your relationship in the depths of a sea of devotion that does not waver just because of waves of difficulty on the surface. Emotional passion doesn't diminish when you or your sweetheart gains ten pounds, or when one of you becomes seriously ill, or even when you aren't getting what you think you should from each other for a while. Together, you ride the sometimes rough surf of life, secure in the knowledge that no storm can wash away the eternal truth of your love.

_____

*It is in the passion of the heart
where the strength of your love
will reveal itself.*

*Passion that lasts cannot be based
on attraction to a physical body
that is always changing.*

*True passion emanates from your soul,
which recognizes its mate in another
and rejoices in the miracle
of your reunion.*

_____

Finding the Time
for Passion

Recently, during the question and answer session at the end of one of my lectures, a couple stood up and shared their dilemma about experiencing more passion in their marriage. *"We want more moments of passion,"* they admitted, *"but we both work long hours, we have two small children, and a lot of the time, we're too tired to have sex as often as we used to. What can we do?"*

This probably sounds painfully familiar to you if you're in a long-term relationship. Perhaps you've even secretly wondered if something is wrong with you or your marriage because you aren't making love as often as you think you should. *"If I really loved him or her like I used to,"* you ask yourself, *"wouldn't I want to have sex more often?"*

The answer is: not particularly. There are many reasons couples find themselves making love less frequently, and the fact is that many of those reasons have little or nothing to do with the lovers' feelings for one another, and more to do with the reality of life. Life takes time; life is tiring; life constantly surprises us with sudden emergencies and deadlines, with projects and children and health issues that demand immediate attention. These hurdles do not care how long it's been since you and your husband had sex. They aren't concerned with how tired or emotionally drained they make you. They appear because they are a part of the drama of this world.

So the first part of the solution is: *Relax.* You're not alone. You're not abnormal. You and your partner are simply human, and doing the best you can to balance your commitment to your family, your careers, yourselves, your community, and your relationship, not an easy feat. You're probably also dealing with a long list of psychological issues that are working themselves out in the marriage, and like it or not, these always affect your life in the bedroom.

How can you deal with all of this? *Start focusing on the quality of your passion rather than the quantity.* Perhaps you can't expect to have the same kind of active sex life you had in the first phase of your relationship, the same quantity. But you can and should expect quality in your physical intimacy, quality that makes each lovemaking session truly special, truly meaningful.

For instance, maybe before you had kids you used to make love twice a week, and now you make love once or twice a month. At first, that may seem like an alarming drop in frequency! But if you approach those times with reverence, as important, sacred occasions when you and your partner can celebrate and express your love and commitment to one another, then each of them will be just as significant and perhaps even more nourishing than the "might as well" sex you used to have every other night.

Here's another point to remember: *Don't limit your expressions of passion to the bedroom.* Sexual intimacy is just one way to show your passion for your beloved and for the gift of your relationship. You can express your passion with words in a card or love note; you can express your passion through considerate acts, such as offering to take care of the children so your wife can have a half hour to herself, or giving your husband a quick shoulder rub when he comes home from work; you can express your passion by inviting your mate to the movies, or by putting on one of your favorite songs and asking her to dance.

Do not wait until you have the time to be physically intimate to express your passion. Don't save it up for some future occasion! *Start by finding at least one moment every day in which you fully express your passion for the person you love. Then, find another, and another.* Before you know it, your relationship will reverberate with passion, and when you do get around to having sex, you'll discover that you've already been making love long before you got into bed!

―――――――

*In the very instant your passion
expresses itself,
whether through an embrace,
a sweet glance,
or an act of kindness,
you enter into the timeless world
of the heart.*

*It does not matter
what has happened before.
It does not matter what will happen next.*

*All that matters is this moment.
All that matters is love.*

―――――――

Stop Waiting for Passion to Find You

Commitment creates passion, not only in our work, or our creative life, but especially in our intimate relationships. To feel passionate about the person you love, you must first feel a genuine commitment to him or her. The passion in love that I'm talking about isn't pure physical passion, or lust—after all, some people can feel that type of fleeting passion with a stranger, so it's no great achievement. The true passion I'm referring to includes the physical, but goes way beyond it. It's the emotional passion that arises when you commit yourself completely to loving another person.

Unfortunately, many of us think it's going to happen the other way around—we think, "I'll make more of a commitment when I feel more passion." And we wonder why things aren't the way we want them to be, why we feel okay in the relationship, but not great, and chalk it up to lack of compatibility. Perhaps we care deeply about someone, and even want to make more of a commitment, but are waiting for a huge explosion of passion in our hearts as a sign that, indeed, *this* is the perfect partner.

What we don't see is that it's the act of holding back in our hearts that's preventing the very experience of passion we're looking for. While you're waiting for passion to find you, your passion is waiting for you to find it.

For this very reason, we must be careful whenever we arrive at a point in a relationship during which we are questioning our commitment to it. Although these times of self-examination are often necessary and healthy, we must remember that the very act of pulling back from our commitment will affect the level of passion we feel. If we are reevaluating our relationship, it's important to factor in the knowledge that the process itself is going to diminish our passion for this person. Then, we can make our decisions based on other more substantial and unchanging elements of compatibility such as friendship, respect, common goals, and a mutual desire to make the partnership work.

Practice committing to what is *working in a relationship, rather than focusing on what's not working.* You may discover that the very act of commitment opens your heart to levels of love and passion you didn't think were possible. Your commitment itself has the power to bring healing to the rough spots in your relationship, and build new bridges of hope, certainty, and connection.

*Don't wait for your passion
to find you.
Create a fertile field in which
true passion can easily grow.*

*Commit yourself as completely
and genuinely as you can
to your relationship.*

*The power of your commitment
will nourish the seeds of passion
and allow it to blossom
in your heart.*

Sabotaging Your Search
for a Passionate Relationship

Some people can't get into a serious relationship because they have a difficult time committing to anyone, and complain that they never seem to find the "right" person. "I just don't feel that special chemistry that tells me she's the one," we say. "I want to feel passionate about someone, I really do, but somehow, it never gets to that point." Wouldn't we be surprised to discover that it may be our own resistance to commitment itself that is sabotaging our search for lasting love?

Continually looking for what's not right about a potential partner doesn't allow room for commitment to grow and passion to blossom. Passion grows in a positive environment, and is suffocated by criticism and faultfinding. If you focus on what's wrong with a person rather than what's right about him or her, you run the risk of never making even the kinds of small commitments that are the foundation for true passion and intimacy.

I'm not suggesting that you make a lifelong commitment to someone you hardly know and don't feel much for in hopes that it will create instant passion. However, in most cases, just expanding your commitment to whatever level of the relationship you do enjoy will open the door for the passion that is there to emerge.

*Look passionately for the good
in each person.
If you look, you will find it.*

*Then, it will not matter
if you end up
spending only twenty minutes with him,
or twenty years.*

*The time you share will be a time of love,
because you looked for the love,
because you found the love.*

Discovering the Passion
of Devotion

When most of us hear the word "passion," we think of sex. It is true—sexual passion is a powerful sensation, the delicious experience of love as it expresses itself in the body. But how sad that many people limit their experience of passion to what occurs for a few moments during sexual intimacy.

Passion is not the same as pleasure. You can experience pleasure without being emotionally involved in what's happening, without being passionate. That's because the source of pleasure is in the physical, in your skin, your nerves. Pleasure is a physical response to certain stimuli, a response that can be turned on or off fairly quickly and easily.

Passion, however, isn't so easy to create or to comprehend. It cannot be turned on and off like a sensation, because it is much more than a sensation. True passion isn't bound by the physical, nor is it confined to what we feel in certain parts of our body. Its source transcends the form, and is found in the formless, in the secret chamber of the heart.

The heart is the home of true passion. There, in the mysterious, invisible realm from which all feeling emerges, the ocean of passion lies waiting to be stirred, not by the right touch or by a skillful caress, but by the one thing that can cause passion to rise up—the love from another heart.

Love is the magic key that unlocks the door to your passion, love that goes beyond the body, the senses, and the ego. It is not dependent upon what mood you are in, how your lover looks that day, whose turn it is to walk the dog, or how much, from moment to moment, you agree with one another. It is love that emerges when you are able to give yourself completely to another, to allow his love to penetrate you as yours penetrates him.

This kind of love has its foundation in devotion—an exalted state of love that recognizes and celebrates the intrinsic oneness of your spirit and the spirit of your beloved. Your bond is ancient, eternal, unbreakable. When you are blessed with this highest form of love, it will express itself with delight in the highest form of passion, passion that turns mere connection into union, and mere physical pleasure into emotional and spiritual ecstasy.

Passion that transcends the body occurs
when your whole being
is passionate about someone else.

Your mind is passionate about his mind.
Your heart is passionate about his heart.
Your spirit is passionate about his spirit.

Every cell in your body vibrates
with passion for your beloved.

This is the passion of devotion.

Keeping the Passion
of Love Alive

Imagine that you've decided to build a fire, perhaps while you're camping, or at home in your fireplace. You carefully choose the logs, the kindling, and after lighting a match to start the fire, you watch over it until you're sure the fire is burning strongly and steadily. Then, you sit back and enjoy the comforting warmth, the delightful play of the flames, the magical light. You don't need to be as vigilant about keeping the fire blazing, since it has enough fuel for now. But at some point, when you notice it's getting a little colder, or the light is growing dim, you realize that the fire needs your attention again. And so you rouse yourself from whatever you've been doing and add more wood, or adjust the position of the logs so that, once more, the flames can rise high.

Even if you've neglected the fire for a while, even if it appears to have died out, you see that the embers still radiate a deep, orange glow that can only be created by hours of extreme heat. The embers are deceptive, and contain great power within their quiet light. Although by themselves they produce no flames, they can ignite a

newly added piece of wood in seconds, suddenly rekin-
dling the full force of the fire, transforming the dormant
coals into a roaring blaze.

We can learn a lot about the passion between two
lovers by thinking about what we intuitively know about
building and maintaining a fire. When you first meet
someone and fall in love, you carefully court and seduce
him or her, adding the right amount of intimacy, the
perfect amount of commitment until the fire of passion
flares up between your hearts and your bodies. For a
while, this blaze burns brightly on its own and you grow
accustomed to the joy it brings into your life. "How lucky
we are," you tell yourself, "to have such a passionate relationship!"

But one day, you realize that there is less light, less
heat between you and your mate, and that, in fact, it's
been that way for some time. You don't feel the same
intense degree of physical attraction, the same desire to
unite, the same stimulation you once felt with each other.
"The passion is gone," you may conclude. "I guess I've
fallen out of love. This relationship is over."

How many people ask themselves, at this critical
point in a love affair, if the fire of passion has died down
simply because no one has been tending it, because no
one has added the fuel necessary to keep it burning? How
many people walk away from the smoking embers of their
marriage, certain that the fire has died out, without notic-

ing that the coals of love still contain enough heat to reignite into flames, if only they are given a chance?

Respect the fire of passion, the fire of love. Understand that to stay alive, it needs to be honored, to be cared for, to be tended as diligently as you would tend a fire you had built in the wilderness to help keep you warm and safe from harm. Feed the fire of your love with kindness, communication, appreciation, and gratitude, and it will always blaze strong and brightly for you.

Passion is the sound love makes
when it sings,
the movement love makes
when it dances.

Passion is the gift you earn
when you honor the fire of love
and learn to keep it burning.

PART THREE

LIVING WITH
PASSION

The Courage to Live Passionately

It takes courage to live passionately. When you choose to live with passion, you open yourself fully to each moment and to each situation. You give everything. You hold nothing back.

This kind of courage isn't the same as the courage it takes to hike for miles in the wilderness, or dive out of a plane with a parachute on your back, or ski down a steep mountain. These feats all require physical bravery, physical courage. The courage to be passionate, on the other hand, doesn't come from confidence in the strength of your body—it comes from confidence in the strength of your spirit.

Spiritual courage is born of faith, not in something on the outside, but faith in yourself, in the inner power you possess that will provide you with everything you need on the next step of your journey. This faith allows you to participate 100 percent in whatever you are doing and wherever you are going. You aren't saving some of your passion for a time in the future when you will be absolutely certain about how things will turn out. You are offering all of who you are to life right now.

In this way, living with passion means living on the edge. *Passion moves you out of your comfort zone into a place of risk, of adventure, of daring. You meet the circumstances and challenges of your life boldly.* It's not that you don't feel doubt or fear—it's that your passion is stronger than your fear. It allows you to see beyond that which is in the way of your dreams, your desires, your destiny, and to go forward with enthusiasm.

I'll never forget an encounter I once had with someone who had made a judgment about my intense enthusiasm and passion for life. *"You know, you can't be for real,"* he said accusingly. *"You're too positive, too excited about what you do. It has to be fake. People just aren't that way."*

I remember feeling amazed as I listened to this man who I knew had been searching unsuccessfully for his own purpose in life. How sad that, to him, anyone who was really excited about life must be faking it. And yet, unfortunately, his point of view is not uncommon in our society where for many, to be "cool" and politically correct means to act like you don't care, to be cynical and sarcastic, to be dispassionate.

The only person's opinion that is going to matter to you at the end of this lifetime is yours. Dare to push past your fear of how you look to others and do what makes you look great to you. Dare to live your life passionately. The world is waiting for your magnificence to unfold.

You have the power to create
a life of deep fulfillment.
You have the power to create
a life of great purpose.

That power lies in your passion.

Find the courage to bring your passion
with you wherever you go.

Find the courage to show your passion
to whomever you meet.

When you choose to be passionate
about your life
your life will be passionate about you.

Passion and Work

Most of us will spend at least one half of our waking life at work, either inside or outside the home. That is a lot of time to spend doing something unless doing it makes us happy. So many people complain that their work isn't fulfilling to them, that they dread waking up in the morning and going to the office. What they're really saying is that their job doesn't allow them to feel any passion.

It's impossible to feel bored, purposeless, and even resentful day after day, week after week, without suffering severe consequences to our psyche. *When we work without passion, we quickly get "burned out."* Fatigue, depression, anxiety, addictions—all these are signs that your spirit is hungry to feel passionate about your work, and frustrated at not feeling fully alive for so many hours each day.

Part of the problem is that we often have rigid notions of what kind of careers one can feel passionate about, and what jobs are just "jobs," a way to make a living and that's it. For instance, you may believe that it's easier to feel passion for work that is glamorous, such as being in the entertainment industry, or for work that pays a lot of money, such as being an investment banker, than it is to feel passion for being a secretary or a salesperson. But remember—the source of passion is within you, and not within a particular kind of job. *It's not the job that makes you passionate. It's you who make your experience of the job come alive by infusing it with your passion.*

Ultimately, this is the secret for finding fulfillment with your work: It really doesn't matter what you do in the world to make a living. *What does matter is how you do it.* You could have the most exciting, high-paying job imaginable, but if you can't find some passion for your work, you'll end up feeling restless, miserable, and unfulfilled. On the other hand, if you choose to express the passionate part of your being by giving 100 percent to a job, even though it's not flashy or doesn't pay a large salary, you will feel a deep sense of satisfaction about what you're contributing to the world, and a sense of peace within yourself.

Do your work with love.
Do your work with gratitude.
Do your work with passion.

This is your true career here on earth,
and you can do it anytime,
and anywhere.

When you give all of yourself
to each moment of your work
and each moment of your life,
you will experience true success,
and you will know true fulfillment.

Seeing the World With Passionate Eyes

Passion isn't just available for people who have lots of money and free time, people who don't have kids and carpools and deadlines and sales meetings and piles of laundry that should have been done last week. It's meant for you. In fact, it's meant for everyone. That's because to experience passion, you don't need glamorous circumstances, or exciting distractions. *All you need to do is learn to see the world with new eyes, with passionate eyes.*

Think back to a time when you first fell in love with someone. Remember how beautiful the world looked to you, how fresh and new everything appeared? The sunsets seemed more breathtaking, the trees and flowers seemed more colorful, the night sky seemed more stunning. In reality, nothing on the outside had changed at all from before you met your beloved. What was different? YOU! Falling in love had connected you with your own passion, and you were seeing the world with new, passionate eyes.

Passion isn't accessible in some sunsets, some evening walks, some bouquets of flowers and not in others. The source of the passion has nothing to do with the objects or even the people you come across. *You bring or do not bring your own passion to each experience. It is your own passion for life that enables you to perceive the true beauty in each person, each setting, each spectacle of nature, each situation you encounter.*

Seeing the world with new, passionate eyes means seeing the world as a lover would. "Did you notice those two birds?" lovers point out to each other. "They were flying so close together—they must be in love." "Isn't it amazing how the wind is caressing the branches of these trees, like it's making love to them?" they marvel. Lovers look for reflections on the outside of their own ardent emotions on the inside. They easily perceive the love, the passion in creation because those are the glasses they are wearing. *They feel love, so they see love. They feel passion, so they see passion.*

In this same way, as you go through your day, look for the love, look for the passionate way life expresses itself:

Instead of just noticing the light appearing outside your window, signaling the start of another busy day, think about how grateful you are to wake up and find yourself alive, to be faithfully greeted by the sun, to be promised another twenty-four hours in which to learn, to laugh, to love.

Instead of simply seeing just piles of waiting laundry, think about your precious loved ones who wear these clothes, who play in them, work in them, sleep in them, and how blessed you are to have these companions in your life.

Instead of just trying to gulp down your meal as quickly as possible so you can get back to work, think about all the people who spent months planning for, carefully growing and harvesting this food so that when you were hungry, you would have something to eat, and think about how fortunate you are to always have enough.

When you begin to see the world in this way, through passionate eyes, each day will be filled with wonder and each moment will be filled with meaning.

When you are in love with life,
you see the world
through the eyes of a lover.
You perceive the world
through eyes of passion.

Seeing with passionate eyes
means noticing the beauty in everything,
marveling at the magic in every moment,
and looking for the love in everyone.

Your Passion Makes a Difference in the World

Once while traveling by plane to a lecture, I sat next to a salesman who was returning home from a hard week on the road. We chatted for several hours about our work, our families, our favorite places in the world to visit, and our dogs! Toward the end of the conversation, this man turned to me with great sincerity and said, "I have a confession to make—I really envy you."

"Why?" I asked.

"Well, I'm just a salesman," he replied. "But you, you really contribute something to the world with your work. You touch people's hearts. If I didn't have all my family responsibilities, I'd quit my job right now and go back to school to get a degree in some helping profession like yours. But even though I know it's too late for that, I can't help but wish I'd done more with my life, that I'd done something really meaningful."

I looked at this warm, thoughtful man, and reflected on how much I'd enjoyed our time together, how much his words and stories had touched me, and said, "Thank you for being honest with me, but I want you to know:

You're wrong!! You *have* done something wonderful with your life. In fact, you've been doing it for the last two hours. You're a passionate, caring person, and that passion has definitely contributed something valuable to my life. You've shared wonderful anecdotes about your family that made me stop and appreciate my family even more. You've described places you've been with so much richness and love that I felt some sweet moments of gratitude for the beauty of God's creation. Your love has made a difference in my life, and I'll bet that every day, your love and your enthusiasm makes a difference in the lives of so many people."

My traveling companion's eyes met mine, and I saw that his were filled with tears. "Thank you," he whispered in a hoarse voice. "I really needed to hear this. I've been feeling like a failure lately, beating myself up because I haven't done enough for the world. I haven't done anything I felt was really significant. And until now, I've never thought about how my passion for life actually contributes to others. But I know you're right, because your passion just made a big difference to me."

No matter who you are,
no matter how you spend your time,
each day you have
dozens of opportunities
to make a difference in the lives
of the people around you
whom you know,
as well as the people you don't know.

How?
By allowing your natural passion for life
to express itself
through your words, your eyes,
your actions
and even through the silent language
of the heart.

Your passion acts like
an invitation to others,
beckoning their own passion
to come forth.

Have Faith in Your Passion

To live and love with passion, you must have faith, faith in your own heart, faith in your own love. Faith means acknowledging the passionate connection you have to your own dreams, your own hopes, your own desire to make a difference in this world. Faith is the natural expression of your passion—when you are passionate about a relationship, a project, or a cause, a feeling of faith rises up in your heart, faith that you will do whatever it takes to make that which you care about a success.

Some people misinterpret the act of having faith as a loss of power, as a relinquishing of responsibility for your life to something outside of yourself. That's dependence, not faith. *Faith doesn't mean relying on something or someone else to rescue you or to make everything all right. True faith is faith in yourself, not in fate.* It is faith in your own inner power, your own passion. It is this passion that motivates you to take charge of your own future, and your faith emerges from your commitment to do so.

The Universe has faith in you, or you wouldn't be here.

87

You have already been given everything you need to fulfill your destiny. Now, it's up to you to take the gift of your life and your uniqueness and share it passionately with others.

It is out of passion that faith is born.

When you surrender to your passion
for happiness, for fulfillment, for truth,
you automatically connect to
the source of life inside yourself.

Suddenly, you feel infused with strength,
with purpose,
with something far greater
than what you previously experienced
as your self.

Then you realize
that faith has nothing to do with hope—
it is a confidence, a knowingness
that Universal Intelligence is working
through you as you.

The Passionate
Universe

We are living in a very passionate universe. If you take a careful look around, it's obvious that whoever or whatever is responsible for creating our physical world did so with a lot of passion. Nature is bold and diverse in its design and detail, indicating to us that the cosmic artist behind the scenes has access to an infinite supply of passion, of enthusiasm, of joy.

Think about it—is it really necessary for there to be thousands of varieties of flowers, in every imaginable shape, in every lovely shade of color, in every intoxicating fragrance? God could have just created a generic flower that would be useful for insects. There really wasn't a need for such a wild display of imagination. What is the explanation for this rainbow of beauty we see in our gardens? Passion! The passion of creative intelligence to express itself with daring, to delight in its own love.

Everywhere in the physical universe, we see this same passionate signature. Each day begins and ends with a spectacular pageant in the sky of purples, oranges, pinks, and reds as the sun rises and sets. Each night we are able to witness a million sparkling stars, like distant diamonds decorating the heavens.

We are alternately entertained, exhilarated, frightened and soothed by sweet breezes, strong winds, fierce storms, steamy heat, cool snowflakes, and refreshing rain. No two clouds are ever identical. No two trees ever grow to be exactly alike. No two waves ever rise and fall in the same spot. Each impressive mountain, each meandering river, each human being has its own uniqueness that cannot be duplicated. And since every living thing is different from every other, each moment is truly unpredictable, always interesting, and never, never boring.

The passionate universe challenges us to live passionately, to meet each new experience with passion, to encounter each new person with passion, to appreciate each of the wonders around us with passion. We are surrounded by constant, magical reminders of how passion manifests itself, as nature lovingly beckons us to join in the passionate dance of life.

Look around you at our miraculous,
glorious world.
Everywhere you will see beauty
that calls out to your own passion.
Everywhere you will perceive majesty
that reminds you of
your own magnificence.

When you allow yourself
to truly view creation in all its splendor,
then you will awaken to the inevitability
of your own power, your own passion,
for you are a part of the splendor.

It is as if God is saying, "I love you.
I am passionate about you.
And that is why I made all this for you."

Sharing Your Gift
of Passion

How can we ever repay that which created us for the blessing of this amazing life? If there is a way, I believe it is to live every moment we have been given fully, completely, and with passion. And living passionately means bringing your love to everyone you meet, and everything you do.

Your love is the greatest gift you can offer to the world. When you share your love, whether in small ways or profound ways, you are sharing your most precious possession. This sharing of something so valuable honors the receiver; it honors yourself as the giver; and it honors the Source from which that love came.

Today, tomorrow, and every day to follow, you will have hundreds of opportunities to share the gift of your love—with a touch or a smile, through a kind word or a compassionate thought, in obvious ways, in invisible ways, with people you know, with people you will never know. Open your heart. Let the river of your passion rush forth. Before long, you will discover the most astonishing secret: *The more love you give away, the more love you'll have!*

Love acts like a radiant light,
illuminating whatever it touches,
kindling the light in each heart
with its own.

The more you love,
the more you live with passion,
the more you give others permission
to do the same.

In this way,
the gift of your passion gets passed on
from person to person,
from heart to heart,
over and over and over again.

Isn't this a miracle?

There will never be an end
to the effect your love has
on the world. . . .